WEDDED WONDERS:
THE WORLD'S MOST AMAZING WEDDING TRADITIONS

BOOK DESCRIPTION:

Step into a world of love, celebration, and timeless traditions with Wedded Wonders: The World's Most Amazing Wedding Traditions. This captivating journey takes readers through the fascinating history of the wedding ceremony and beyond, exploring over 100 of the most unique and remarkable wedding customs from cultures across the globe.

From ancient rituals passed down through generations to modern-day ceremonies that break all conventions, Wedded Wonders unveils the beauty and diversity of how love is honored around the world. Discover:

The history of weddings, tracing how this sacred ceremony evolved from practical alliances to grand celebrations of love.

More than 100 wedding traditions, each more intriguing than the last, such as underwater weddings in Thailand, Maasai beaded collars in Kenya, and Game of Thrones-inspired nuptials.

Exquisite wedding feasts, highlighting the most amazing dishes served at wedding banquets, from fermented shark in Iceland to lobster and phoenix chicken in China.

Breathtaking wedding outfits, showcasing the rich cultural meanings behind bridal attire—from the bold colors of Indian saris to the elegant Norwegian bridal crowns.

Unforgettable modern weddings, featuring hot air balloon ceremonies in Turkey, Northern Lights celebrations in Norway, and rollercoaster weddings for thrill-seekers.

Whether you're planning your own wedding or simply fascinated by global cultures, this book will broaden your horizons and inspire you with fresh, unusual ideas. Wedded Wonders is not only a window into the world's most extraordinary wedding celebrations, but also a reminder of how love transcends borders, with each tradition offering something truly magical to the timeless union of two people.

Discover, be inspired, and maybe even find your own "something borrowed" from these incredible wedding traditions!

CONTENTS OF THE BOOK:

CHAPTER 1: THE TRADITION OF CELEBRATING WEDDINGS

The tradition of celebrating weddings dates back thousands of years, evolving alongside different cultures, religions, and societal norms. While it's impossible to pinpoint a specific time or place where the very first wedding celebrations occurred, marriage itself as a formal union has existed in nearly all human societies for millennia. Early wedding traditions varied greatly based on local customs, but over time, common elements like feasting, rituals, and ceremonies emerged.

Let's take a journey through the history of wedding celebrations to understand how they began, their significance, and how they transformed over time.

Ancient Origins of Marriage Ceremonies
1. Prehistoric and Early Human Societies (before 3000 BCE)

In early human societies, the concept of marriage was likely informal and primarily functional, focusing on the alliance between families, reproduction, and the pooling of resources. There is evidence of early human unions being celebrated through simple rituals, but these were more focused on the practical aspect of bonding people into cooperative units rather than romantic love. These unions were often arranged by families or tribes for survival and to ensure the continuation of the group.

2. Ancient Mesopotamia (c. 3000 BCE)

The earliest documented evidence of formal marriage ceremonies comes from ancient Mesopotamia, specifically from the Sumerians. Marriage in these societies was a legal and economic agreement between families. The bride and groom were often accompanied by elaborate contracts involving dowries and gifts between families.
The wedding ceremony included:
Contracts and gifts: Weddings were transactional, with the groom paying a dowry to the bride's family, and the bride bringing a dowry of goods or land.
Feasts: Celebrations after the contract was signed, often involving food and communal feasts.
Priestly blessings: In some cases, the union was blessed by a religious figure.
Marriage was less about love and more about economic stability, family alliances, and reproduction. However, the idea of celebrating the union did emerge in the form of communal feasts and ceremonial rites.

3. Ancient Egypt (c. 3000 BCE)

In ancient Egypt, marriage was a social and legal contract that strengthened the bonds between families. Weddings were not elaborate ceremonies but rather private, informal events. The couple's family played a significant role, and there was no priest or formal authority to sanction the marriage. However, some symbolic rituals, such as exchanging gifts, feasting, and offering sacrifices to the gods, marked the union.

Feasts and gifts: Both families would exchange gifts and celebrate with food and music.

Divine connection: Marriage was seen as sanctioned by the gods, particularly through rituals that invoked blessings from deities like Hathor, the goddess of love.

4. Ancient Greece (c. 1200 BCE – 600 BCE)

In ancient Greece, marriage was a central institution, vital for producing legitimate heirs. The wedding process was extensive and involved several stages:

Engagement ceremony: Known as engye, this was a formal agreement between the groom and the bride's father.

Procession and rituals: The wedding ceremony, called gamos, involved a procession where the bride was taken to the groom's house in a decorated chariot, followed by sacrifices and a communal feast.

Hymeneal songs: Songs were sung to the Greek god Hymen, the god of marriage, to bless the union.

Weddings in ancient Greece were more public and ceremonial, and while the marriage was still transactional, it started to incorporate more social elements like dancing, singing, and feasting.

5. Ancient Rome (c. 753 BCE – 476 CE)

Marriage in ancient Rome was also about family alliances and property. Roman wedding ceremonies (confarreatio) were steeped in religious and legal formalities, and often involved rituals that symbolized the union of the couple.

Key elements included:

Rituals with deities: The bride and groom would make offerings to the gods, especially Juno (the goddess of marriage).

Joining of hands: This act symbolized the legal and personal bond between the couple.

Feasts: Roman weddings were followed by elaborate feasts, and it was customary to end with the phrase "Feliciter," meaning "good luck."

Roman weddings also included a public procession, where the bride was escorted to her new home, and the groom pretended to "steal" her from her family, symbolizing the transition from her father's household to her husband's.

The Middle Ages (5th – 15th Century)

As Christianity spread throughout Europe, marriage traditions were increasingly influenced by religious customs. The church began to formalize and oversee marriage ceremonies, making them more of a religious sacrament rather than just a legal or social contract.

1. Christianity's Influence on Marriage

By the 12th century, the Catholic Church had declared marriage one of the seven sacraments. Church ceremonies became the standard for many people, and the blessing of the union by a priest was essential. These weddings were no longer just contracts but divine unions sanctioned by God.

Key elements of medieval Christian weddings:

Church ceremonies: Weddings were held in churches and included prayers, blessings, and vows exchanged in front of God.

The exchange of vows: Couples began to recite vows, promising fidelity, care, and love for each other.

Feasting and music: After the church service, there was often a large community feast, with food, drink, dancing, and music.

2. Royal and Noble Weddings

Medieval royal and noble weddings were extravagant affairs. They were highly political, as marriages were often arranged to form alliances between powerful families or nations.

Large celebrations: Royal weddings featured grand feasts that lasted for days, with dancing, tournaments, and entertainment.

Symbolism and pageantry: The bride's dowry and gifts exchanged were often symbols of wealth and power.

The Renaissance and Early Modern Period (15th – 18th Century)

By the Renaissance, weddings began to evolve further. Marriages were still arranged, but there was a growing emphasis on love and companionship, especially among the wealthy and aristocratic classes.

1. Renaissance Weddings

Weddings in Renaissance Europe became more about the pageantry, with elaborate costumes, public processions, and ceremonial displays. Wedding garments were often luxurious, and the celebrations could last for several days.

Love and companionship: The Renaissance also saw the rise of courtly love, and while most marriages were arranged, the idea of romantic love began to influence marriage traditions.

Bridal attire: White wedding dresses, while not yet the norm, became more common for wealthy brides as symbols of purity and status.

2. Protestant Reformation

In the 16th century, the Protestant Reformation brought changes to marriage practices, particularly in countries that broke away from the Catholic Church. Marriage became less about religious sacraments and more about personal vows, with ceremonies often held outside the church. However, communal celebrations like feasts, dancing, and gift-giving remained central.

Victorian Era (19th Century)

The Victorian era (1837-1901) introduced many wedding traditions that are still in practice today. Queen Victoria herself set the stage for modern weddings by wearing a white wedding dress, popularizing this fashion.

1. White Wedding Dress

Before Queen Victoria, brides often wore their best dress, regardless of color. But after her 1840 wedding, the white dress became a symbol of purity, innocence, and wealth. This tradition quickly spread through Europe and beyond.

2. Elaborate Ceremonies

Weddings became more elaborate in the Victorian era, with a stronger focus on romantic love, family values, and propriety. Ceremonies were often held in churches, followed by grand receptions with formal dinners, speeches, and dancing.

3. Honeymoons

The concept of the honeymoon also gained popularity in the Victorian era. Wealthy couples would often take a "bridal tour," visiting friends and family before embarking on a romantic journey together.

Modern Weddings (20th Century Onward)

The 20th century saw a global convergence of wedding traditions, influenced by mass media, global travel, and changes in societal values. The rise of personal choice in marriage, love-based unions, and diverse cultural practices all played a role in shaping contemporary weddings.

1. Romantic and Love-Based Marriages

By the early 20th century, romantic love became the primary reason for marriage in many parts of the world, particularly in the West. Weddings became more personal, with couples choosing to write their own vows and customize their ceremonies.

2. Wedding Customs and Trends

Wedding rings: The tradition of exchanging rings became universal, symbolizing eternal love.
Bridal party: Bridesmaids and groomsmen became common, and bachelor and bachelorette parties developed as pre-wedding traditions.
Reception and parties: Modern weddings typically feature large receptions with formal meals, speeches, dancing, and cake-cutting ceremonies.
Destination weddings: Couples increasingly chose exotic locations for their wedding ceremonies, creating a new trend of "destination weddings."

Today's Weddings

Weddings today are a blend of old and new, with

traditions from various cultures coexisting with modern trends. Couples now have more freedom to design ceremonies that reflect their personalities, preferences, and values, whether incorporating age-old rituals or creating entirely new ones.

Inclusivity and diversity: Modern weddings celebrate diversity, with multicultural ceremonies and non-traditional marriages, including same-sex weddings.

Personalization: Many couples now tailor their weddings with unique touches—writing personal vows, choosing non-traditional venues, and planning ceremonies that reflect their values and tastes.

Technology and social media: Technology has transformed weddings, with live-streamed ceremonies, social media hashtags, and digital wedding invitations.

Summary

The tradition of celebrating a wedding began as a practical and often transactional agreement in early human societies, evolving into a more ceremonial and celebratory event over time. Ancient cultures like the Sumerians and Egyptians focused on marriage as a legal or familial bond, while the Greeks and Romans introduced more elaborate rituals and feasts. The spread of Christianity brought marriage into the religious domain, with weddings becoming sacraments celebrated in churches.

By the Renaissance and Victorian periods, weddings became more romanticized, with the white dress, formal vows, and honeymoons becoming common.
In the modern era, weddings have continued to evolve, with an emphasis on love, personal expression, and cultural fusion.
Today, weddings are a blend of ancient traditions and contemporary practices, reflecting both the history of the institution and the evolving values of modern society.

CHAPTER 2: WEDDING TRADITIONS AROUND THE WORLD

Wedding traditions around the world are deeply rooted in cultural practices, history, and values, offering fascinating insights into different societies.

Here's a list of interesting, unusual, and amazing wedding traditions from various peoples around the world:

AFRICA

Kenya (Masai) – Spitting on the bride: The father of the bride spits on her head and chest for good luck before she leaves with her husband.

South Africa – Fire rituals: The couple's parents bring fire from their hearths to light the couple's new home.

Nigeria (Yoruba) – Knocking on the door: The groom and his family "knock" at the bride's family home, symbolically asking for her hand in marriage.

Sudan (Nuer) – Cattle dowry: The groom must give cattle to the bride's family and only when the wife has two children does the marriage become fully legitimate.

Ghana – Kente cloth: Couples wear beautifully woven, brightly colored Kente cloths during the ceremony to symbolize heritage and unity.

Ethiopia – The groom shows his strength by holding

a sword while dancing, which signifies protection and power.

Morocco – Bridal henna night: A ritual to protect the bride from evil spirits, with intricate henna designs applied to her hands and feet.

Egypt – Zaffa: A lively, drum-led parade with belly dancers and bagpipes, announcing the arrival of the bride and groom.

Tunisia – Seven-day celebration: Couples celebrate for seven days before the wedding, with each day dedicated to a particular event.

Congo – No smiling allowed: The couple is not allowed to smile throughout the ceremony to show they are serious about the union.

ASIA

India (Hindu) – Saptapadi: The bride and groom take seven sacred steps together around a fire, symbolizing their journey together.

Pakistan – Rukhsati: After the wedding, the bride says an emotional goodbye to her family and leaves for the groom's home.

China – Shooting the bride: The groom shoots three arrows (without heads) at the bride, which he then breaks to ensure lasting love.

Japan – San-san-kudo: The couple takes three sips from three sake cups during a Shinto wedding to symbolize union and commitment.

South Korea – Wooden ducks: The groom gives his bride a pair of wooden ducks or geese, symbolizing fidelity and lifelong partnership.

Mongolia – Chicken liver test: Couples must kill a chicken and inspect its liver to choose a wedding date. If the liver is good, the date is chosen.

Indonesia (Java) – Tooth filing: The bride and groom's teeth are filed down in a symbolic ritual to rid them of evil spirits and bad luck.

Malaysia – Colorful threading: During the wedding ceremony, threads of different colors are tied around the couple's wrists to symbolize unity.

Vietnam – Tea ceremony: Both families gather in a tea ceremony, where tea is offered as a symbol of respect and unity

Philippines – Dove release: During the ceremony, the bride and groom release two doves into the air, symbolizing peace, prosperity, and love in their marriage.

Thailand – Water pouring: Guests pour water over the couple's hands while offering blessings for happiness, health, and wealth in their marriage.

Cambodia – Sword dance: A sword dance is performed by the groom's side to protect the bride and ensure the strength and unity of the marriage.

Nepal – Marrying a fruit: In some communities, the bride marries a fruit, symbolizing her temporary marriage to a deity before her union with the groom.

Sri Lanka – Thali tying: The groom ties a sacred

necklace (Thali) around the bride's neck, symbolizing their union and the bride's new status as a married woman.

Tibet – Yak butter sculptures: Intricate sculptures made from yak butter are used during wedding ceremonies as offerings to the deities for blessings.

EUROPE

Scotland – Blackening of the bride: Friends of the bride cover her with soot, feathers, and flour before the wedding to prepare her for any hardships she may face in marriage.

Ireland – Claddagh rings: Couples exchange Claddagh rings, which depict two hands holding a heart, symbolizing friendship, love, and loyalty.

Germany – Log sawing: After the ceremony, the bride and groom saw a log together to demonstrate their ability to work as a team in their future life.

Norway – Bridal crown: The bride wears a silver or gold crown adorned with small charms that are meant to ward off evil spirits.

Sweden – Kissing tradition: If the groom leaves the room during the reception, the male guests line up to kiss the bride, and vice versa.

Greece – Stepping on bread: The couple steps on a piece of bread as a sign of their willingness to provide for each other.

Italy – Breaking a vase: The bride and groom break

a vase, and the number of pieces is believed to predict how many years of happiness they will have.

France – Croquembouche: The traditional wedding cake is a tower of cream-filled pastries held together by caramel, symbolizing prosperity.

Poland – Oczepiny: During the reception, the bride removes her veil and tosses it to unmarried women, symbolizing the passing on of good luck.

Hungary – Bridal dance: Guests pay to dance with the bride by placing money in her shoes, which helps the couple start their new life together.

Romania – Bride kidnapping: Friends of the groom "kidnap" the bride, and the groom must negotiate her return with her friends by offering gifts or money.

Denmark – Cutting off the groom's socks: After the ceremony, guests cut off the groom's socks to symbolize that he is now tied down and can no longer "walk away."

Iceland – Viking wedding: In some weddings, couples incorporate Viking traditions like wearing traditional Norse clothing and exchanging ceremonial swords.

Spain – Arras coins: The groom gives the bride 13 coins, known as arras, symbolizing his commitment to provide for her and their future family.

Finland – Sauna wedding: Some Finnish couples get married in a sauna, which is considered a sacred space in Finnish culture, symbolizing purification.

MIDDLE EAST

Lebanon – Zaffe: A lively pre-wedding procession filled with drumming, dancing, and music to celebrate the union of the bride and groom.

Turkey – Henna night: The night before the wedding, the bride's hands and feet are adorned with henna to protect her from evil spirits.

Israel (Jewish) – Breaking the glass: At the end of the ceremony, the groom breaks a glass underfoot to remind the couple that marriage is a balance of joy and sorrow.

Palestine – Zajal: The wedding features traditional Palestinian music and chanting, often in the form of a poetic duel between two performers.

Iran – Sofreh Aghd: The couple sits in front of a beautifully decorated spread of symbolic items like sugar cones, which are ground over the couple's heads to bring sweetness to their marriage.

Saudi Arabia – Sword dance: The groom and his male family members perform a sword dance to mark the beginning of the wedding celebration.

Yemen – Bridal canopy: A tent is set up around the bride during the ceremony to symbolize her new home and her protection within her marriage.

Jordan – Sugar throwing: Guests throw sugar at the bride and groom to bless them with a sweet and prosperous life.

Oman – Perfume and incense: The couple is showered with perfumes and incense during the ceremony, as it is believed to bring good luck and happiness.

LATIN AMERICA

Mexico – Lazo ceremony: A large rosary or silk cord (lazo) is placed around the couple's shoulders in a figure-eight shape, symbolizing the unity and eternal bond between them.

Peru – Cake pull: Charms attached to ribbons are hidden between the layers of the wedding cake. Each single woman pulls a ribbon, and the woman who pulls the one with the ring is said to be the next to marry.

Brazil – Bridal shoes for money: The bride's shoes are placed on a table, and guests drop money into them to help the couple start their married life.

Colombia – Gold coins (arras): During the ceremony, the groom gives the bride 13 gold coins, representing Christ and the apostles, as a symbol of his commitment.

Argentina – A ribbon ring game: Similar to Peru, ribbons are placed inside the cake with one ribbon attached to a fake ring. The woman who pulls the ribbon with the ring is believed to be the next bride.

Cuba – Money dance: Guests pin money to the

bride's dress while dancing to help the couple with wedding expenses or to begin their life together.

Chile – Engagement ring on the right hand: Couples wear their engagement rings on their right hands and move them to the left after the ceremony.

Ecuador – Holy water blessing: The bride and groom are often blessed with holy water during the ceremony, symbolizing purity and divine protection.

Bolivia – Crucifix exchange: Couples exchange crucifixes during their wedding ceremony as a symbol of faith and commitment.

Guatemala – Breaking of a bell: The mother of the groom breaks a white ceramic bell filled with rice, flour, and grains to bring prosperity to the couple.

North America

United States (Southern tradition) – Burying the bourbon: In Southern states, the couple buries a bottle of bourbon upside down at the wedding site to ward off bad weather.

United States (Native American Navajo) – Cornmeal ritual: The bride and groom often participate in a cornmeal ceremony where they exchange cornmeal to honor their ancestors and connect with the earth.

Canada – Bridal toasts: Guests give impromptu toasts or "roasts" of the bride and groom, offering humorous stories and advice.

Haiti – Wedding coins: Similar to other Latin

American traditions, the groom presents 13 coins to the bride, representing Christ and his disciples.

Jamaica – Wedding parade: After the ceremony, there's often a community parade where friends and family escort the couple, accompanied by loud music and dancing.

Bahamas – Junkanoo wedding: Inspired by the Bahamian Junkanoo festival, weddings often include colorful parades with masks, music, and vibrant dancing.

Mexico (Mayan tradition) – Xuc ceremonial dance: A traditional dance known as "Xuc" is performed at weddings to honor Mayan heritage and ancestors.

Honduras – Crowning the bride: The bride is crowned with flowers, symbolizing purity and beauty, during the ceremony.

Belize – Jankunu dancers: Couples often incorporate Jankunu dancers, who wear elaborate costumes and masks, into the wedding celebrations as a form of entertainment.

Dominican Republic – Bridal dolls: A doll dressed in a replica of the bride's gown is placed on the head table, symbolizing the bride's role as the new head of her family.

Australia and Oceania

Australia – Stone ceremony: The couple and their guests each hold a stone, which they place in a communal vessel. This ritual signifies the support of family and friends in their union.

New Zealand (Maori) – Haka dance: The groom and his groomsmen perform the Haka, a traditional Maori war dance, to display strength and unity.

Fiji – Whale tooth gift: In Fiji, the groom must present the bride's father with a tabua (whale's tooth) as a gesture of respect and intent to marry.

Samoa – Tapa cloth: The bride and groom are often wrapped in tapa cloth, made from bark, which symbolizes their unity and their family's blessings.

Tonga – Ngatu ceremony: The bride is wrapped in a ceremonial cloth called "ngatu" as a sign of her connection to family and tradition.

Papua New Guinea – Pig exchange: Pigs are often exchanged between families as part of the dowry, symbolizing wealth and the merging of the two families' resources.

Tahiti – Matting ceremony: The couple is wrapped together in a ceremonial matting as a symbol of their union and their shared life.

Vanuatu – Traditional kava ceremony: Before or after the wedding, the couple drinks a beverage made from the kava root in a traditional ceremony that symbolizes unity and peace.

Solomon Islands – Shell money dowry: In some regions, shell money is used as a form of dowry, given by the groom's family to the bride's family as a sign of respect and unity.

Hawaii – Lei exchange: The bride and groom

exchange leis, symbolizing their love and commitment, as well as their connection to nature and Hawaiian tradition.

EASTERN EUROPE

Ukraine – Korovai bread: The wedding bread, "korovai," is a richly decorated loaf shared by the couple, symbolizing prosperity, fertility, and unity.

Poland – Blessing with bread and salt: The bride and groom are presented with bread, salt, and wine by their parents as a symbol of prosperity, the hardships of life, and joy.

Lithuania – Tossing coins: The groom throws coins into the crowd during the wedding procession, and guests try to catch them as a sign of good luck and wealth.

Latvia – Veil dance: At midnight, the bride's veil is removed, and she dances with all the married women, symbolizing her transition into married life.

Bulgaria – Breaking bread over the couple's heads: A loaf of bread is broken over the couple's heads during the wedding reception to bless them with prosperity and fertility.

Hungary – Choosing godparents: During the wedding ceremony, the couple chooses two godparents who will guide them through their married life.

Romania – Ceremonial kidnapping: Friends of the bride "kidnap" her during the reception, and the groom must "rescue" her by performing tasks or paying a ransom.

Slovakia – Wedding wreath: Instead of a veil, the bride wears a wreath made from flowers or ribbons, symbolizing her purity and connection to nature.

Georgia – Swords and wine: A traditional wedding often involves the groom using a ceremonial sword to open a wine barrel, symbolizing strength and celebration.

WESTERN EUROPE

Spain – Orange blossoms: Brides wear orange blossoms in their hair or on their dress, symbolizing purity and eternal love.

Portugal – Bride's bouquet auction: The bride's bouquet is auctioned off to the guests, with the proceeds often going toward the couple's honeymoon or charity.

Italy – La tarantella dance: Couples and guests participate in a lively dance known as the "tarantella," symbolizing happiness and good fortune for the newlyweds.

France – Charivari: A noisy gathering of friends and family outside the couple's home on their wedding night, banging pots and pans to "disturb" the couple and demand drinks or treats.

Germany – Polterabend: Friends and family break dishes the night before the wedding, and the bride and groom must clean them up together, symbolizing teamwork.

Austria – Stealing the bride: Guests "kidnap" the bride during the reception, and the groom must find her and negotiate her return by buying drinks for everyone.

Belgium – Handkerchief: The bride's family presents her with a personalized handkerchief, embroidered with her name, which she keeps as a family heirloom.

Netherlands – Tree planting: The couple plants a tree together to symbolize their growing love and the life they will build together.

Switzerland – Log sawing: The couple saws a log together after the ceremony to demonstrate their teamwork and commitment to overcoming obstacles in their marriage.

Luxembourg – Candle lighting: The couple lights a candle together during the ceremony to symbolize their unity and the brightness of their future.

South and Central Asia

Bangladesh – Coconut smashing: The groom's family smashes a coconut on the ground to bring good luck and remove obstacles from the couple's path.

Nepal (Newar community) – Bel fruit marriage:

Before marrying their human spouse, Newar girls are married to the bel fruit (wood apple) in a ceremony that signifies their eternal marriage to the god Vishnu.

Maldives – Traditional Maldivian boat (dhoni) wedding: Couples get married on a traditional Maldivian dhoni boat, symbolizing their journey together.

Sri Lanka – Poruwa ceremony: The couple stands on a beautifully decorated platform called a "poruwa," and rituals involving betel leaves, coconut flowers, and coins are performed to bless their union.

Afghanistan – Henna night: Like many cultures, Afghani brides have a henna night before the wedding to bless the bride and protect her from evil spirits.

Bhutan – Exchange of scarves: The bride and groom exchange white scarves called "khatas" during the ceremony, symbolizing purity and their new life together.

Uzbekistan – Bread-cutting ceremony: The couple shares bread at the wedding as a symbol of their new life together, offering blessings of abundance.

Kazakhstan – Bride's dowry display: The bride's dowry, including handmade items, is displayed before the wedding to show the wealth and skill of the bride and her family.

Tajikistan – Seven blessings: Seven rounds of

blessings are given to the couple during the ceremony by family members and elders, wishing them happiness, prosperity, and long life.

Kyrgyzstan – Wedding on horseback: In rural areas, the groom rides to the bride's house on horseback, symbolizing a traditional nomadic wedding.

CHAPTER 3: THE MOST UNUSUAL AND INTERESTING WEDDING DISHES FROM DIFFERENT COUNTRIES

Wedding feasts around the world are filled with unique and culturally significant dishes, some of which may seem unusual or surprising to people outside of the culture. These dishes are often chosen for their symbolic meanings or to honor long-standing traditions.

Here are some of the most unusual and interesting wedding dishes from different countries:

1. China – Dragon and Phoenix

In Chinese weddings, it's common to serve dishes that symbolize prosperity, happiness, and harmony. One such dish is the "Dragon and Phoenix," which refers to lobster (representing the dragon) and chicken (representing the phoenix). These two creatures symbolize the balance between male and female energies. The lobster and chicken are often prepared in elaborate ways and served with various sauces and side dishes.

2. Philippines – Balut

Balut, a fertilized duck egg with a partially developed embryo, is a popular snack in the Philippines. While it may seem unusual to outsiders, it is sometimes served at wedding banquets in the Philippines as a delicacy. Balut is considered a symbol of strength and fertility, making it an apt dish for such celebrations.

3. Greenland – Kiviak

In Greenland, a traditional dish served at weddings is Kiviak, which is made by fermenting whole seabirds (usually auks) inside a seal skin. The seal skin is sewn shut and buried under stones for several months, during which the birds ferment. Kiviak is an acquired taste, to say the least, but it is considered a delicacy and is often served at Greenlandic weddings as part of their Inuit heritage.

4. South Africa – Mopane Worms

In some parts of South Africa, particularly among rural communities, mopane worms are a delicacy that can be included in wedding feasts. These large, protein-rich caterpillars are typically dried or fried and then served as a crunchy snack. The worms are highly nutritious and are sometimes included as a cultural nod to traditional foods.

5. Japan – Tako Wasabi (Octopus with Wasabi)

At Japanese weddings, a variety of fresh seafood is often served. One unusual dish is Tako Wasabi, which consists of raw octopus marinated in a spicy wasabi sauce. It's served as a cold appetizer, and though it may seem unconventional, it's considered a delicacy in Japan and adds a unique touch to wedding feasts.

6. Scotland – Haggis

In Scotland, haggis, a savory pudding made from sheep's organs (heart, liver, and lungs) mixed with oatmeal, onions, and spices, is often featured in wedding celebrations. It's traditionally served with "neeps" (turnips) and "tatties" (potatoes). Although haggis might seem strange to outsiders, it is a beloved dish in Scottish culture, symbolizing national pride and culinary tradition.

7. Iceland – Hákarl (Fermented Shark)

Icelandic weddings sometimes feature Hákarl, which is fermented Greenland shark meat. The preparation process involves burying the shark to ferment it for several months, after which it's dried and served in small pieces. It has a very strong ammonia-like smell and taste, and though it's considered unusual or even extreme, it's a traditional delicacy in Iceland.

8. India – Goat Head Curry

In some regions of India, especially in southern states like Tamil Nadu, goat head curry is considered a delicacy and is often served at weddings. The head of the goat is slow-cooked with a blend of spices, and the resulting dish is rich, flavorful, and considered auspicious.

9. Finland – Kalakukko (Fish Pie)

Kalakukko is a traditional Finnish dish sometimes served at weddings, particularly in rural areas. It's a fish pie made with fish (usually perch or salmon), pork, and bacon, all encased in a thick rye dough and baked for several hours. While it may seem unusual to have a fish pie at a wedding, it's a beloved dish that symbolizes Finnish hospitality and tradition.

10. Kenya – Nyama Choma (Grilled Meat)

In Kenya, Nyama Choma, or roasted/grilled meat, is a popular dish at weddings. The meat (usually goat, beef, or chicken) is grilled over an open flame and served with side dishes like ugali (maize porridge) and kachumbari (a fresh tomato and onion salad). While grilled meat isn't unusual in itself, the way it's prepared and served whole in communal settings is unique to Kenyan celebrations.

11. Norway – Smalahove (Sheep's Head)

Smalahove, a dish made from the head of a sheep, is sometimes served at traditional Norwegian weddings, particularly in rural areas. The sheep's head is salted, smoked, and boiled or steamed, then served with potatoes and mashed rutabaga. It's a dish with deep historical significance in Norway, though it may seem unusual to outsiders.

12. Sweden – Surströmming (Fermented Herring)

In Sweden, Surströmming, fermented Baltic herring, is sometimes served at weddings as part of a traditional Swedish smorgasbord. The fish is fermented for several months and has a very strong odor, which many people find challenging. However, it's considered a delicacy and is often eaten with flatbread, potatoes, and onions.

13. Mongolia – Boiled Sheep's Tail

In Mongolia, boiled sheep's tail is considered a delicacy and is often served at weddings and other special occasions. The fatty tail of the sheep is prized for its flavor and texture, and it's considered a symbol of abundance and prosperity in Mongolian culture.

14. Madagascar – Romazava

In Madagascar, Romazava is a traditional dish served at weddings, consisting of a stew made from beef, pork, and leafy greens (typically cassava leaves). What makes it unusual is the inclusion of tiny wildflowers that give the stew a unique taste and aromatic quality. The dish is often served with rice, and it holds cultural significance as a communal meal symbolizing unity.

15. Yemen – Saltah

In Yemen, Saltah, a stew made from meat, vegetables, fenugreek froth, and spices, is sometimes served at weddings. What makes it unusual is the addition of a layer of frothy, beaten fenugreek on top of the stew. It's served with flatbread and symbolizes hospitality and the sharing of food, a core value in Yemeni culture.

16. Tonga – Lo'i Feke (Octopus in Coconut Cream)

At traditional Tongan weddings, Lo'i Feke, octopus cooked in coconut cream, is a delicacy often served to guests. The octopus is stewed until tender and mixed with a rich coconut sauce, which is a staple in

Pacific Island cuisine. While octopus may not seem strange, the preparation method and cultural significance make it unique to Tongan wedding feasts.

17. Peru – Cuy (Guinea Pig)

In some Andean regions of Peru, Cuy (roasted guinea pig) is served at special occasions, including weddings. Guinea pig is considered a delicacy and has been eaten for centuries in the Andes. The meat is typically roasted whole and served with potatoes or corn, and while it may seem unusual to outsiders, it's a significant dish in Peruvian culture.

18. Malaysia – Nasi Minyak

In Malaysian weddings, Nasi Minyak (oily rice) is a common dish. It's cooked with ghee, spices, and herbs, giving it a fragrant aroma and rich flavor. While rice is a staple across Asia, what makes Nasi Minyak unique is its deep, rich flavor and its role as a celebratory dish in Malay weddings, symbolizing abundance and happiness.

19. Uzbekistan – Plov

In Uzbekistan, Plov is a wedding staple. It's a rice dish cooked with mutton, carrots, onions, and spices, and is prepared in large quantities for wedding feasts. The dish is considered unusual for its grand scale and the elaborate preparation process, with some weddings serving Plov from massive communal pots, symbolizing hospitality and generosity.

20. Greece – Kokoretsi

Kokoretsi is a traditional Greek dish served at some weddings, consisting of lamb or goat intestines wrapped around seasoned organ meat (like liver, hearts, and lungs) and grilled on a spit. While it may seem unusual to some, Kokoretsi is a beloved dish in Greece and is often prepared for special occasions like weddings and Easter celebrations.

CHAPTER 4: WEDDING ATTIRE AROUND THE WORLD

Wedding attire around the world varies widely depending on cultural traditions, religious beliefs, and local customs. Some wedding outfits may seem unusual or striking to those unfamiliar with the culture, yet each has a deep significance and history.

Let's explore some of the most unusual and fascinating wedding outfits from different countries:

1. Japan – Traditional Kimono with Tsunokakushi

In traditional Japanese Shinto weddings, the bride wears a white silk kimono called shiromuku, symbolizing purity and a new beginning. What makes this outfit unusual is the tsunokakushi, a white hood the bride wears to cover her hair. The tsunokakushi is meant to hide the bride's "horns of jealousy," symbolizing her intent to become a gentle and obedient wife.

Groom's attire: The groom wears a traditional black kimono with a family crest, called montsuki, and hakama (wide-legged pants).

2. Mongolia – Deel and Headdress

Mongolian wedding outfits are among the most intricate and unique. The bride and groom both wear a traditional outfit called a deel, a long silk robe that is richly decorated. The bride's outfit is often adorned with ornate headpieces, sometimes featuring wide, wing-like extensions called khalkhas, which symbolize status and beauty.

Headgear: The bride's elaborate headdress includes silver ornaments and coral beads, symbolizing wealth and fertility. The groom also wears a distinctive hat with a red ribbon, symbolizing protection.

3. Nigeria – Aso-Oke and Gele

In Nigeria, particularly among the Yoruba people, brides often wear a traditional handwoven fabric called Aso-Oke. This fabric comes in bright, bold colors, often with intricate patterns, and is considered a symbol of wealth and heritage.

Gele: The most striking part of the outfit is the gele, a large, elaborate headwrap worn by the bride. The groom's attire, usually made from similar fabric, includes a agbada, a wide-sleeved robe.

4. Scotland – Kilt and Tartan

In Scottish weddings, the groom traditionally wears a kilt, a knee-length skirt-like garment made of woolen cloth in a tartan pattern representing the groom's clan. What's unusual about this outfit is the formality of the kilt combined with accessories like a sporran (a small pouch worn around the waist) and sgian-dubh (a small ceremonial knife).

Bridal attire: The bride sometimes incorporates the groom's tartan into her outfit by wearing a sash or shawl.

5. India – Lehenga and Sherwani

Indian wedding attire is known for its vibrant colors and intricate details. The bride traditionally wears a lehenga (a long, embroidered skirt) or a sari, often in shades of red, which symbolizes prosperity and fertility. The fabric is richly adorned with gold thread, beads, and sequins.

Groom's attire: The groom typically wears a sherwani (a long, coat-like garment) along with a safa (turban). What's unusual about the groom's attire is the sehra, a curtain of flowers or beads that covers his face.

6. South Korea – Hanbok

In traditional Korean weddings, the bride and groom wear hanbok, traditional Korean clothing. The bride's hanbok is a bright, voluminous outfit with long sleeves and a high waist, often decorated with colorful embroidery.

Hwarot: The bride may also wear a traditional royal robe called hwarot, embroidered with symbols of longevity, happiness, and wealth, along with a large headdress adorned with jade and gemstones.

7. Ghana – Kente Cloth

In Ghana, the bride and groom often wear matching kente cloth garments at their wedding. Kente is a handwoven cloth with bold, geometric patterns and bright colors, each design having its own meaning.

Significance: The use of Kente cloth in weddings represents a connection to Ghanaian heritage, royalty, and the union of the two families.

8. Indonesia (Java) – Batik Sarong and Kebaya

Javanese brides and grooms wear traditional batik garments made from intricately dyed fabric with geometric or floral patterns. The bride's outfit often includes a kebaya, a long-sleeved lace blouse, and a batik sarong.

Hair and headpieces: The bride wears her hair in a traditional style called paes ageng, with her forehead painted in black patterns. She may also wear a gold or floral headpiece called sanggul.

9. Kenya (Maasai) – Beaded Jewelry and Shúkà

In Maasai weddings, both the bride and groom wear a traditional cloth called a shúkà, often in vibrant red, symbolizing protection and bravery. What makes this attire unique is the elaborate beadwork that adorns the bride.

Beaded collars: The bride wears a large, circular beaded necklace that covers her entire chest and shoulders, symbolizing beauty, strength, and the Maasai people's connection to their ancestors.

10. Bhutan – Gho and Kira

In Bhutan, the groom wears a gho, a knee-length robe tied at the waist, while the bride wears a kira, a long, rectangular piece of silk wrapped around her body.

Traditional scarves: Both the bride and groom wear colorful scarves during the wedding, called rachu (for women) and kabney (for men), symbolizing their new status as a married couple.

11. Norway – Bunad

In Norway, some brides choose to wear a bunad, a traditional Norwegian folk costume, which is often handmade and varies by region. The bunad is a woolen dress that includes intricate embroidery, metal buckles, and silver jewelry.

Bridal crown: The bride may wear a silver or gold bridal crown decorated with small charms that are meant to protect her from evil spirits.

12. Russia – Kokoshnik

In traditional Russian weddings, brides sometimes wear a kokoshnik, a tall, beaded headpiece. This headpiece is richly decorated with pearls and beads and is a symbol of Russian heritage and beauty.

Sarafan: The bride may also wear a sarafan, a long, flowing jumper dress, though in modern times it is often combined with contemporary wedding styles.

13. Malaysia – Baju Kurung and Songket

In Malaysia, the bride wears a traditional baju kurung (a long tunic with a skirt), or baju kebaya, often made from luxurious songket, a handwoven fabric with gold or silver threads. The intricate patterns on songket symbolize prosperity and good fortune.

Tudung: Muslim brides often wear a tudung, a headscarf or veil, to signify modesty and respect, often embellished to match the wedding outfit.

14. Tibet – Robes with Turquoise Jewelry

Tibetan brides and grooms wear layered robes made from silk or wool, depending on the weather and region. What makes Tibetan wedding attire unique is the extensive use of turquoise and coral jewelry, which holds religious and cultural significance.
Jewelry: The bride's jewelry is elaborate, with necklaces, earrings, and headdresses made of turquoise, coral, and silver, symbolizing protection and wealth.

15. Sri Lanka – Kandyan Saree and Mul Anduma

In Sri Lankan weddings, particularly among the Sinhalese, the bride wears a Kandyan saree, a long draped garment with pleats, while the groom wears a traditional costume called Mul Anduma. The groom's attire features a short jacket with a ceremonial sarong and a striking headdress.
Seven necklaces: The bride wears seven necklaces, symbolizing wealth and prosperity, along with elaborate hair ornaments.

16. Romania – Traditional Folk Costumes

In some rural regions of Romania, brides and grooms wear traditional folk costumes at their wedding. These outfits are heavily embroidered with intricate patterns that vary by region and often feature bright colors like red, green, and gold.
Veil and headscarf: The bride's veil is often replaced with a headscarf, signifying her transition into married life.

17. Hungary – Wedding Headdress (Pártá)

In Hungary, brides traditionally wear a headdress called pártá, a large, ornate crown made of ribbons and flowers. The headdress is often brightly colored and serves as a symbol of the bride's virginity.
Veil-changing ceremony: During the wedding, there is often a veil-changing ceremony, where the bride's traditional headdress is removed and replaced with a veil, signifying her new role as a married woman.

18. Peru (Quechua) – Ponchos and Hats

In traditional Quechua weddings in Peru, both the bride and groom wear colorful ponchos. The bride's outfit may include a brightly colored skirt and a montera (a wide-brimmed hat), while the groom's poncho is often adorned with woven patterns that symbolize his heritage.
Woven belts: The bride and groom wear special woven belts that signify their connection to the earth and agricultural life.

19. Samoa – Tapa Cloth Wedding Dress

In Samoa, brides wear dresses made from siapo or tapa cloth, a traditional fabric made from the bark of the mulberry tree. The dress is often decorated with intricate hand-painted patterns, and it symbolizes the connection to Samoan heritage and nature.
Headdress: The bride may also wear a pale, a large crown made from shells and flowers, symbolizing beauty and purity.

20. Morocco – Kaftan and Heavy Jewelry

In Moroccan weddings, the bride often wears a kaftan, a long, flowing gown made from luxurious fabrics like silk or velvet. The kaftan is richly embroidered with gold or silver thread, and the bride may wear multiple outfits throughout the wedding celebration.

Heavy jewelry: The bride wears a significant amount of gold jewelry, including necklaces, bracelets, and earrings, to symbolize wealth and prosperity.

CHAPTER 5: MOST UNUSUAL AND AMAZING MODERN WEDDINGS FROM AROUND THE WORLD

Here's a collection of some of the most unusual and amazing modern weddings from around the world, each told like a story. These weddings reflect the creativity and personality of couples, while blending tradition with contemporary trends.

Let's explore how love is celebrated in unique ways today!

1. An Underwater Wedding – Thailand

Picture this: A bride in a flowing white gown and a groom in a sharp suit, but instead of walking down an aisle, they're swimming through the turquoise waters of Thailand. In the small town of Trang, couples have been getting married underwater for years. Certified divers exchange vows beneath the sea, surrounded by coral reefs and schools of fish. The ceremony is just like any other—there are vows, rings, and kisses—but with one twist: everything happens underwater! The couple and their officiant wear scuba gear, and they even hold waterproof signs to display their vows. This unique setting brings an element of adventure and serenity, as bubbles rise with each word they speak. After the ceremony, they emerge from the water to celebrate with family and friends on the beach, marking the occasion with traditional Thai festivities, dancing, and feasting.

2. A Game of Thrones-Inspired Wedding – United States

In the heart of America, one couple turned their love for Game of Thrones into an epic wedding event. Picture this: a forested landscape, mist swirling around as the guests arrive in medieval-inspired attire. The bride walks down the aisle in a flowing gown reminiscent of Daenerys Targaryen, while the groom stands at the altar dressed like Jon Snow, complete with a faux fur cape.

The ceremony takes place under a towering weirwood tree, with a handfasting ritual—an ancient Celtic tradition where the couple's hands are bound together with ribbons—symbolizing their union. For the reception, there's a grand feast with roasted meats, ale, and, of course, a towering cake in the shape of a dragon. Candlelit tables, rustic wooden benches, and live medieval music set the mood. This wedding wasn't just a celebration of love, it was a journey into a fantasy world, where every detail, from the goblets to the throne-like chairs, felt like it was pulled straight from Westeros.

3. A Wedding in a Hot Air Balloon – Turkey

In the fairy-tale-like region of Cappadocia, Turkey, where the sky is filled with colorful hot air balloons every morning, one couple decided to take their wedding to new heights—literally. As dawn breaks, the bride and groom step into a large hot air balloon basket, surrounded by close family members.

As they gently lift off, the breathtaking landscape of Cappadocia's rock formations stretches out beneath them. Floating thousands of feet above the ground, the couple exchanges vows in mid-air. Their officiant stands with them, and as they say "I do," the sky is painted with the pinks and oranges of sunrise. After landing, a celebratory breakfast awaits them on the ground with local Turkish pastries and tea, turning a simple meal into a magical post-wedding feast.

4. A Silent Disco Wedding – United Kingdom

In a bustling city in the UK, a couple with a love for music—and a desire to keep the neighbors happy—decided to have a wedding reception like no other: a silent disco! Picture this: a dance floor filled with guests, each wearing wireless headphones, dancing wildly but in complete silence. The twist? Everyone can choose their own music channel.

As the bride and groom take to the dance floor for their first dance, everyone watches quietly as they sway to their chosen song. Then, when the party begins, guests switch between playlists—some listening to classic hits, others choosing modern pop or even hip-hop. If you take off the headphones, you hear nothing but laughter, footsteps, and the occasional off-key singing. This modern take on a wedding party ensures that everyone can enjoy the music they love without the noise complaints.

5. A Pop-Up Wedding – Australia

Imagine planning a wedding without the stress of months of preparation, endless guest lists, or seating charts. In Australia, pop-up weddings are becoming a modern trend. One couple decided to have their dream wedding in this minimalist yet chic style. Here's how it works: The couple chooses a location—whether it's a beach, a park, or an urban rooftop. On the day of the wedding, a pop-up wedding company arrives and sets up everything within an hour. There's an elegant arch, simple chairs for guests, and fresh flowers that perfectly match the setting. The ceremony is short but sweet, focusing on the couple's love story. The best part? After saying their vows, they have a mini photo shoot, share a toast with their closest family and friends, and then leave for a spontaneous honeymoon. It's all about simplicity, but with elegance and meaning, proving that love doesn't need extravagance to be special.

6. A Zero-Waste Wedding – Canada

In the scenic mountains of Canada, one environmentally conscious couple wanted a wedding that reflected their love for each other and the planet. They planned a zero-waste wedding, where everything from the invitations to the food was designed to leave no waste behind.

Instead of paper invites, guests received digital invitations. The bride wore a vintage wedding dress passed down through generations, and the groom opted for a suit he already owned. The decorations were made from local, biodegradable materials—think wildflowers, leaves, and recycled fabric. The food was sourced from local farms, served on reusable plates, and any leftovers were donated to a local shelter. Even the flowers were repurposed after the wedding, turned into compost or given to guests as gifts. It was a celebration not only of their union but of their commitment to a sustainable future.

7. A Heli-Wedding – New Zealand

In the dramatic landscape of New Zealand, a couple with a love for adventure decided to tie the knot in a way that matched their thrill-seeking personalities. Their wedding took place on the top of a remote mountain, accessible only by helicopter.

The day begins with the bride and groom stepping into a helicopter, dressed in full wedding attire. As they soar through the skies, the rugged peaks of the Southern Alps come into view. The helicopter lands on a snow-capped mountain, where the couple steps out into the crisp, fresh air. There, surrounded by nothing but the beauty of nature, they exchange vows. The ceremony is intimate, with just a few guests who also flew in by helicopter. After the wedding, the couple takes off again, enjoying a scenic flight over glaciers and lakes before returning to the ground for a relaxed celebration with friends and family.

8. A Rollercoaster Wedding – United States

For one fun-loving couple, getting married in a church wasn't nearly thrilling enough. They chose to exchange their vows on a rollercoaster! At a theme park in the U.S., the couple, along with their wedding party, strapped in for the ride of a lifetime.

As the rollercoaster slowly ascended, the officiant, seated in the front row, quickly read the vows. Just as the couple said their "I do's," the rollercoaster plunged into its first drop, and their first kiss as a married couple happened while hurtling through the air at high speeds! After the ride ended, they celebrated with carnival food, cotton candy, and games, turning the entire theme park into their wedding reception. For these two, their wedding was about joy, fun, and a little bit of adrenaline.

9. A Northern Lights Wedding – Norway

In the remote wilderness of Norway, one couple planned a winter wedding that would coincide with one of nature's most spectacular shows—the Northern Lights. They traveled with their guests to a lodge deep within the Arctic Circle, where the ceremony took place outdoors under the vast, starry sky.

The bride wore a fur-lined cape over her dress to keep warm, while the groom was dressed in a thick wool coat. As they exchanged vows, green and purple lights began to dance across the sky—an unforgettable backdrop to their intimate ceremony. Afterward, the celebration moved indoors, where guests gathered around a roaring fire, enjoying hearty local dishes like reindeer stew and Arctic char. The Northern Lights continued to shimmer above, making the entire evening feel like a magical, once-in-a-lifetime event.

10. A Wedding on a Glacier – Iceland

In the icy wonderland of Iceland, one adventurous couple decided to say their vows on a glacier. With the towering ice formations as their backdrop, they took a short hike to reach the perfect spot for their wedding.

The bride wore a thick white cape over her gown, and the groom was bundled up against the cold in a tailored wool coat. They stood on the gleaming blue ice as their officiant read the vows. Despite the chill in the air, the moment was warm with love. After the ceremony, the couple and their guests explored the ice caves, then warmed up with a cozy reception in a nearby lodge, enjoying Icelandic delicacies like smoked lamb and skyr, a creamy yogurt-like dessert.

FINAL THOUGHTS:

As you close the pages of Wedded Wonders: The World's Most Amazing Wedding Traditions, I hope you've been inspired by the incredible diversity and beauty of wedding ceremonies around the world. From ancient rituals to modern-day celebrations, each tradition reflects the values, history, and creativity of the people who celebrate love in their own unique ways.
Whether you've marveled at the breathtaking outfits, been intrigued by the unusual wedding dishes, or found yourself captivated by a particular tradition, I hope this journey has broadened your horizons and perhaps sparked ideas for your own special day. Love is universal, but the ways we express it are endlessly diverse—and that's what makes every wedding truly one-of-a-kind.

Your thoughts and feedback are incredibly important to me. I would love to hear what you enjoyed most about this book, which traditions fascinated you, and how this journey through wedding wonders has inspired you. Your feedback helps other readers discover this book and enriches the conversation about the world's most extraordinary wedding traditions.
Please take a moment to share your thoughts and

leave a review. Your voice will help guide others on their own journey through these magical wedding stories, and who knows—your insight might just inspire the next bride or groom to add something extraordinary to their own celebration of love. Thank you for being part of this adventure. I look forward to hearing from you!

With gratitude, Olesia Naumchyk.